BYRON KATIE

on

Health, Sickness, and Death

Edited by Stephen Mitchell

the work of
byron katie
WWW.THEWORK.COM

BYRON KATIE INTERNATIONAL, INC. • LOS ANGELES

Published in the United States by:
Byron Katie International, Inc.
578 Washington Blvd. Box 821
Marina del Rey, CA 90292
1-800-98KATIE (52843)
www.thework.com

ISBN 1-890246-81-6

Printed in the United States of America.
Design & Layout by Balsam Design
Art Director: Richard Balsam
Production Specialist: Emily Eoff
Cover Photography: Brie Childers

With deepest gratitude to all the staff
who have made the School for The Work
possible for so many

The Work of Byron Katie:
The Four Questions and Turnaround

1. Is it true?

2. Can you absolutely know that it's true?

3. How do you react when you believe that thought?

4. Who would you be without the thought? *and*

Turn it around.

Every story is about body-identification.
Without a story, there's no body.

Bodies don't think, care, or have any problem
with themselves. They never beat themselves
up or shame themselves. They simply try
to keep themselves balanced and to heal
themselves. They are entirely efficient,
intelligent, kind, and resourceful. Where
there's no thought, there's no problem. It's
the story we believe, prior to investigation,
that leaves us confused. My pain can't be my
body's fault. I tell the story of my body, and
because I haven't inquired, I believe that my

body is the problem and that if only this or
that changed, I would be happy.

Your body is not your business. If you need
a doctor, go to one. That way you get to be
free. Your body is your doctor's business. *Your*
business is your thinking, and in the peace of
that you're very clear about what to do. And
then the body becomes a lot of fun, because
you're not invested in whether it lives or dies.
It's nothing more than a metaphor for your
thinking, mirrored back to you.

If I lose all my money, good. If I get cancer, good. If my husband leaves me, good. If my husband stays, that's good too. Who wouldn't always say yes to reality if that's what you're in love with? What can happen that I wouldn't welcome with all my heart?

You are my inner life. You're the voice of my self, reporting my health at all times. Sickness or health—it's all fine with me. You're sad, you're not sad; you don't understand, you understand; you're peaceful, you're upset; you're this, you're that. I am each

cell reporting itself. And beyond all change,
I know that each cell is always at peace.

For people who are tired of the pain, nothing
could be worse than trying to control what
can't be controlled. If you want real control,
drop the illusion of control, let life have you.
It does anyway. You're just telling the story
about how it doesn't. That story can never be
real. You didn't make the weather or the sun
or the moon. You have no control over your
lungs or your heart or your ability to see or
walk. One minute you're fine and healthy, and
the next minute, you're not. When we

try to be safe, we live our lives being very, very careful, and we wind up having no lives. I like to say, "Don't be careful: you could hurt yourself."

Bodies don't crave, bodies don't want, bodies don't know, don't care, don't get hungry or thirsty. It's what that mind attaches to—ice cream, alcohol, drugs, sex, money—that the body reflects. There are no physical addictions, only mental ones. Body follows mind. It doesn't have a choice. Actually it's simultaneous, but as long as you are mentally experiencing duality, body follows mind.

What fun is it to be God if I can't get a glimpse of myself in the mirror? And whether I like it or not, that's what I am. I'm vanity— total vanity. So when people are attached to their looks and their health, it's coming from an honest source. It's just misinterpreted. It's pure innocence.

All thoughts that we attach to are about survival, then health, then comfort, then pleasure. Every thought has to be about "I"; that's how you survive. And then as soon as you get your little house, your little car, your little piece of turf, your thoughts turn to the story of how you need to be healthy and comfortable. You get stuff in the shopping cart, you get stuff in the house, and as soon as you're comfortable, your thoughts turn to pleasure. This is full-scale body-identification: there's no thought that isn't about the body. So you go to pleasure when you have your little ducks in order. And all pleasure is pain, because you're worried about losing it, and trying to make it last or to get more of it. You never really experience it, you're always in its past or future.

I once did The Work with a woman who was ashamed of her fingers. She had come down with rheumatoid arthritis when she was seventeen, and afterward she believed that her fingers were deformed. They weren't normal, she thought, and she suffered a lot from that belief. But her fingers *were* normal: they were normal for *her*. They were the fingers she had woken up with every day since she was seventeen. For twenty-seven years they were her normal fingers, and she hadn't noticed. How do you react when you believe that what is isn't normal for you? Shame, sadness, despair. Who would you be without that thought? At ease with your condition and loving it, whatever it is, because you would realize that it is completely normal, for you. Even if 99.99% of other people look a different way, their normal isn't your normal: *this* is your normal. That tree out there, let's go out and give it a talking-to, it's all bent, every branch of it, and I don't think it has a clue that it's not normal. And while we're at it, let's discuss God too, because he made a big mistake, he really botched that tree, it's supposed to grow straight, and let's devote our lives to straightening it out. That kind of argument with reality was what was going on in this dear woman, and that was what caused her suffering, not her fingers.

Give us permission, through you, to have a flaw, because flaws are the norm. When you hide your flaws, you teach us to do that. I love to say that we are just waiting for one teacher, just one, to give us permission to be who we are now, so that we can all come to know that that's what is normal for us. You appear as this now. That's such a gift to give. The pain is in withholding it. Who else is going to give us permission to be free, if not you? Do it for your own sake, and we'll follow. We're a reflection of your thinking, and when you free yourself, we all get free.

It's not ever going to be about food, or alcohol, or drugs, or money, or health. We just keep using symbols to stay body-identified. And eventually nothing holds.

You are the perfect health, whether you like it or not. You tell the story of how you're supposed to be stronger or healthier so that you don't have to know that your condition is perfect. My condition is perfect for what I need to do now, for where I need to be now. I'm without a future.

The body is never our problem. Our problem is always a thought that we innocently believe. The Work deals with our thinking, not with the object that we think we're addicted to. There *is* no such thing as an addiction to an object; there is only an attachment to the uninvestigated concept arising in the moment.

When we're sick, we want people to be kind to us, we want the nurses to be kind to us. And yet we're not being kind to ourselves, because we're lying in bed with an enemy: our disease. Until we are at peace with our worst enemy, which always is our thinking, we can't love our beloved partner or our precious child. Sooner or later, everything we think about our disease will have to be attached to our partner or our child when we don't get our way or when we think we're going to lose something. We don't resist our diseases, we resist our thoughts about them. Without our story, we can't have a problem. We can only have a solution.

Bodies are as innocent as trees or flowers or breath.

There's nothing else to do but get well, and that's not up to the body. Ultimately the body's not going to make it. This is good news—it's over, forget it, let's work with what we do have. Can you get it from here? If this body story were true, it means that no fat person can be self-realized, no one in a wheelchair, no one old or sick, no one who's not beautiful. This leaves out practically the whole human race! Almost no one has a chance for freedom under this theory. We're all waiting until we get it perfect to be peaceful. Can we just do it from here, now?

If it comes to me to take my estrogen, I do it. If it doesn't come to me, I don't do it. So I'm always directed. And they say, "Oh, poor thing, she died because she didn't take her whatever-it-was." Well, *you're* stuck with that story, and I'm free. And so are you if you investigate. Because it's always about the story. That's why it's so wonderful to be sick and to get old. It's wonderful to lose your leg or your arms or your eyes or your loved one. Investigate the stressful thoughts you have about your condition until you see that it's the perfect condition for you.

When you believe your thoughts, you rape
your body by saying that it should be more
beautiful, it should be healthier, it should
be taller, shorter, fatter, thinner, younger,
stronger. You take a perfect body and trash it.

Awareness is so much more exciting than
a body.

My heart's always healthy. Even if it were
having an attack, my heart would be healthy.
It's perfect for that moment. Whether it's

beating strongly or blasting into oblivion,
it's as it should be. If you argue with what's
happening, you have a heart attack with a lot
of fear. But without a story, without arguing
with reality, you can have a heart attack in
peace. "Wow! So this is how she goes out, so
this is how the story ends!" A heart attack can
be very exciting. This is just about awareness.
The awareness of what is: you are that
movement itself. (And not even that.)

When you're asleep, does your body hurt?
When you're in the worst pain, and the phone
rings and it's the call you've been waiting for,

and you're mentally focused on the phone call,
there's no pain. If you change your thinking,
you change the pain.

I was in Holland a few years ago, and I was
running very high fevers. And The Work went
on every day. I was working with people from
early morning to late at night. And I noticed
that a few times, during a break, I would be
just huddled up in a corner, exhausted, with
a high fever, in heaven. My body is not my
business. If you don't tell me I'm sick, I have
no way of knowing. And in the clarity of that,
I always seem to be well. No story, no sickness.

There was snow, there was cold, there was sky, there were people, there was breath, there was fever, there was exhaustion, there was joy—everything! Without a story, I'm free.

How do you live when you believe that your health problems should not be there? You can't even tell us the truth. You can't even cough or blow your nose honestly, or let us know you're not feeling well. Who would you be without the story "I should feel better"? You'd be free.

I love this old age thing. It blows every concept about health. I'm ninety years old and I have arthritis, but "I should move fluidly." I don't think so! That kind of thinking is true masochism. When I say my body should move fluidly, how does that make me feel when it doesn't?

There's no "vibration" that's higher or lower or different. There's only a story that would separate them out. All together there's one vibration. You vibrationally match everything you've got in the moment. And you have everything, so you're a perfect match. "If you had a higher vibration, you'd have better health"—can you absolutely know that that's true? How do you live when you believe that your vibrations are too low to heal your body? Masochism. War. Who would you be without that theory? A little more relaxed, a little more ready for healing.

Bodies don't have the power to take away your peace. I would rather be happy instead, and let the body do what it does.

When you believe that you are this body, you stay limited. That way you get to be small, apparently encapsulated as a body, as one separate form. So every thought has to be about your survival or your comfort or your pleasure, because if you let up for a moment, there would be no body-identification. When you're asleep and dreaming, you're free— you're bodiless, you're a man, a woman, a dog, a tree, you're in the kitchen one moment and on a mountain top the next, or all of it simultaneously, nothing is ever stable because you can't body-identify. It's not limited. It's thoughts without an identification that you can attach to. So every time you notice you're body-identified, put "my thinking" on it.

Or "is it true?" and watch how you become free from the body and its limitations.

Someone said this morning, "You look like you're losing weight." Good. "You look like you're gaining weight." Good. "You look old." Good. "You look young." Good. Body is not my business. My thinking is my business. So watch the masochistic thoughts you believe, to stay body-identified. And have fun!

A peaceful mind doesn't care about a body.

❧

"Your shoulder shouldn't hurt"—is that true?
It hurts exactly the way it does. It *should* hurt
exactly the way it does. It's a flat-out lie that it
shouldn't. Your story is how you keep yourself
in time and space and duality. This is not a
right or wrong. We're looking at reality here.
If you argue with reality, if you lie about what
you know is true, it feels stressful. It opposes
what you are. "It's not supposed to hurt like
this." Feel how painful that thought is. How
many times have you been there? I used to
live in that place. I lived there, in bed, for

years. No wonder you cry when you say, "My shoulder shouldn't hurt this much," because your shoulder should hurt this much. It does. That's reality.

Every belief is about being careful; it's about keeping the body alive. I'm not careful. I don't live that way. Whatever comes, I look forward to it.

If you believe that certain foods are really good for you, and you love eating those foods, and you feel good when you eat them, and it feels like loving yourself, that sounds very sweet to me. It sounds like a peaceful, honest way of living. The war zone starts when you believe that other people should eat that way too: your partner or your children, for example. You can't know what's best for them. Maybe your carrot is their ice cream. You just can't know them. Can you know yourself?

Once I went for twenty-seven days without food. There was no reason; I just knew not to eat. And during all those days, I couldn't find a trace of hunger. It was just another myth.

My family and friends were very fearful for
my life, but I wasn't concerned. I felt healthy
and strong, and I was doing a lot of vigorous
walking the whole time. And at no moment
did I experience anything but myths about
hunger and bellyaches and weight loss. There
was just nothing real. I couldn't find one
legitimate need that didn't come face to face
with the fear of death. And then, after twenty-
seven days, without any reason, I knew to eat.

There's no suffering in the world, there's only
a story that would lead you to believe it.
There's no suffering in the world that's real.

Isn't that amazing? Investigate and come to know for yourself.

Pain is a friend. It's nothing I want to get rid of, if I can't. I'm a lover of what is. It's a sweet visitor; it can stay as long as it wants to. (And this doesn't mean that I won't take the Tylenol.)

"Yoga makes your shoulder feel better"—that's one of your sacred beliefs. Can you really know that that's why your shoulder stopped hurting? When you're focused on your shoulder, focused on "yoga is going to make it better," "massage is going to make it better," "carrot juice is going to make it better," you're body-identified. At night we pass out from these concepts. We don't sleep, we pass out. You're scared of pain in your body. When the carrot juice stops working, you're left with your own thought system. You try to hold it off with yoga. There's only one true yoga, and it's mental, and it's a free flow. I'm a lover of what is. I have played out all these theories, and I know that even if the massage and the yoga and the carrot juice and the wheat grass work now, eventually I'll have the grace of getting old and knowing that the wheat grass

can't help. Or hopefully I'll get some kind
of disease, where all this thought catches up
with me, and I can take a look at my stressful
concepts. It's all grace. And don't you want it
all? Freedom from the body, freedom from
the concept that you are a body. Something's
always going to hurt. Ultimately you're left
with your thinking about your body. That's all
there is to work with.

If you think that alcohol makes you sick or
confused or angry, then when you drink it, it's
as if you're drinking your own disease. You're
meeting alcohol where it is, and it does exactly

what you know it will do. So we investigate
the thinking, not in order to stop drinking,
but simply to end any confusion about what
alcohol will do. And if you believe that you
really want to keep drinking, just notice what
it does to you. There's no pity in it. There's no
victim in it. And eventually there's no fun in
it—only a hangover.

I suggest that you not do The Work with the
motive of healing your body. Go in for the love
of truth. Heal your mind. Meet your concepts
with understanding. I love to say that when you
finally get your body totally healthy, a truck

hits it. So can we be happy from here now, not tomorrow, not in ten minutes—can we be happy right now? I use the word *happy* as in a natural state of peace and clarity, and that's what The Work gives us.

Even physical pain isn't real; it's the story of a past, always leaving, never arriving. But people don't know that. My grandson Racey fell down once when he was three years old. He scraped his knee, and there was some blood, and he began to cry. And as he looked up at me, I said, "Sweetheart, are you remembering when you fell down and hurt yourself?" And immediately, the crying stopped. That was it. He must have realized, for a moment, that pain is always in the past. The moment of pain is always gone. It's a remembering of what we think is true, and it projects what no longer exists. (I'm not saying that your pain isn't real for you. I know pain, and it hurts! That's why The Work is about the end of suffering.)

If a car runs over your leg and you're lying in the street with story after story running through your mind, chances are that if you're new to The Work, you're not going to think,

"'I'm in pain'— is it true? Can I absolutely know that it's true?" You're going to scream, "Get the morphine!" Then, later, when you're in a comfort zone, you can sit down with a pen and paper and do The Work. Give yourself the physical medicine and then the other kind of medicine. Eventually, you can lose your other leg, and you won't see a problem. If you think there's a problem, your Work isn't done.

As long as we believe that we're a body, we don't have to know that we are infinite, our cells without limit, like music, itself, free.

Are you afraid of being incontinent when you're old? Suppose your bowels let go in public—that would be normal for you. There would be no problem unless you believed that there was. When a baby does that, we think it's cute, it's healthy. Who would you be without your story? If it's not okay for your bowels to release any time, anywhere, your Work is not done. That's what bowels are for: everything is for your homecoming. If that's what you need, it's the gift that reality will give you.

Some people believe that if you're physically sick, you aren't spiritual enough, you aren't enlightened enough. If you were enlightened enough, you wouldn't have a stomach ache, for example, or heart disease, or cancer. I don't know about enlightenment, but even when I am ecstatic, my stomach does what it does. And that seems to be how I live. My stomach is not my business; my thinking is my business, and not even that. Even if you have perfect peace, your body does what it does. "Sickness isn't spiritual"—can you really know that that's true?

A doctor once took a sample of my blood and came back to me with a long face. He said he was bringing bad news, he was very sorry, but I had cancer. Bad news? I couldn't help laughing. When I looked at him, I saw that he was quite taken aback. Not everyone understands this kind of laughter. It later turned out that I didn't have cancer, and that was good news too.

The truth is that until we love cancer, we can't love God. It doesn't matter what symbol we use—poverty, loneliness, loss—it's the concepts of good and bad that we attach to

them that make us suffer. I was sitting once
with a friend who had a huge cancerous tumor,
and the doctors gave her just a few weeks to
live. As I was leaving her bedside, she said, "I
love you," and I said, "No, you don't. You can't
love me until you love your tumor. Every
concept that you put on that tumor you'll
eventually put on me. The first time I don't
give you what you want, you'll put that concept
on me." This might sound harsh, but my friend
had asked me to always tell her the truth.
The tears in her eyes were tears of gratitude,
she said.

On one occasion in 1986, while I was getting a massage, I began to experience a sudden paralysis. It was as if all the ligaments, tendons, and muscles had tightened to an extreme. It was like rigor mortis; I couldn't make even the slightest movement. Throughout the experience, I was perfectly calm and joyful, because I didn't have a story that the body should look a certain way or move fluidly. Thoughts moved through, like "Oh my God, I can't move. Something terrible is happening." But the inquiry that was alive within me wouldn't allow any attachment to these thoughts. If that process were slowed down and given words, it would sound like this: "'You're never going to be able to walk again' — sweetheart, can you really know that that's true?" They're so fast, these four questions. Eventually, they meet a thought at the instant of its arising. At some point, after about an hour, my body began to relax and go back to what people would call its normal state. My body can never be a problem if my thinking is healthy.

How do you live when you believe the thought that your body should be different? How does that feel? "I'll be happy later, when my body is healed." "I should be thinner, healthier, prettier, younger." This is a very old religion.

If I think my body should be different from
what it is now, I'm out of my business. I'm out
of my mind!

⤜

Your medicine is whatever appears now.

⤜

How do you know that you need cancer?
You've got it. But to accept cancer is not to
lean back and do nothing. That's denial. You
consult the best doctors you can afford, and
you get the best treatment available. Do
you think your body is going to heal most

efficiently when you're tense and fearful and fighting cancer as an enemy? Or when you're loving what is and realizing all the ways in which your life is actually better because you have cancer, and from that calm center doing everything you can to get better? There's nothing more life-giving than inner peace.

No one even cares if he has cancer. We don't care if we live or die. We just want this mind to stop. And in my experience it's not going to stop—but we can meet it with some understanding, and we can have freedom.

Nineteen years ago a doctor removed a large tumor from my face. I had found inquiry—inquiry had found me—so I didn't have a problem with the tumor. On the contrary: I was delighted to see it come, as I was delighted to see it go. It was actually quite a sight, and before it was removed I loved being out there in public. Everyone would look at it and pretend not to be looking, and I was just the observer of that. Maybe a little girl would stare at me, and her parents would whisper to her and yank her away. Did they think I was some sort of freak? I didn't feel like one. That tumor on my face was normal for me; it was reality. Sometimes I would catch someone looking at the tumor, and he would look away, then after a while he would look again, then look away, look again, then look away. And finally we would both laugh, because since I could see it without a story, eventually he could see it that way too, and it was just funny.

People who are afraid of cancer may think, "If I get spiritual enough, I'll heal my cancer." So they get spiritual, and they go to church or they start meditating for hours a day, and their cancer heals, and they say they did it with their spiritual practice. Can you really know that that's true? Who needs God when you are that spiritual? "I healed my cancer":

that's not the way it works. But as long as
we use our physical bodies to measure our
spiritual evolution, then our monitor is
always the focus, and the real deal
is secondary.

I have a friend who didn't want to take
medication. And I said, "God is everything,
but not medicine?" God is medicine too.
So today she sees that it's a privilege to take
medicine. And whether it's working or not
is not her business. She knows that. The
medicine says, "Take once a day." That's all
she has to know. It's written on the bottle.

"I'm supposed to sleep at three o'clock in the morning"—is it true? I don't think so: I'm wide awake. When I wake up in the middle of the night, I get very excited. What could be better than sleep? Waking! I love lying in bed in the middle of the night with my eyes wide open, because that's what I'm doing. There's no thought that I should be doing anything else. I love all my thoughts.

No one can be too fat or too thin. That's not possible. It's a mythology. It keeps you from the awareness of what is. It's the death of awareness. We don't want it, but we just don't know another way. So we investigate and even in a five-hundred-pound body, we get lighter.

If someone says to you, "You're fat," they're right. Can you find it? And that's a candle over there, what's it going to do—die of shame? Don't call me a woman, or I'll go to war. Or tall. Or short. Do you understand? If someone says, "You should lose weight," I understand that. I've had the same thought myself. I find where they're right, I join them, and I give myself peace.

If I lose my right arm, how do I know I don't need two arms? I have only one. There's no mistake in the universe. To think in any other way is fearful and hopeless. The story "I need two arms" is where the suffering begins, because it argues with reality. Without the story, I have everything I need. I'm complete with no right arm. My handwriting may be shaky at first, but it's perfect just the way it is. It will do the job in the way I need to do it, not in the way I thought I needed to do it. Obviously, there needs to be a teacher in this world of how to be happy with one arm and shaky handwriting. Until I'm willing to lose my left arm, too, my Work's not done.

I'm not asking you to let go of your body, as if
such a thing were possible. I'm asking you to
own your body, to care for it, to take a look
at your beliefs about it, to put them on paper,
inquire, and turn them around.

When the mind thinks of death, it looks at
nothing and calls it something, to keep from
experiencing what it—the mind—really is.
Until you know that death is equal to life,
you'll always try to control what happens, and
it's always going to hurt. There's no sadness
without a story that opposes reality.

When the mind leaves a body, we throw it in the ground and walk away.

What is death? How can you die? Who says that you were ever born? There is only the life of an unquestioned thought. There is only mind, if anything. Live in the four questions for a while. That is where the world ends, until what's left comes back to explore the next concept. Do you continue after death? If you question your mind, you see that what you really are is beyond life and death.

No one knows what's good and what's bad.
No one knows what death is. Maybe it's not
a something; maybe it's not even a nothing.
It's the pure unknown, and I love that. We
imagine that death is a state of being or
a state of nothingness, and we frighten
ourselves with our own concepts. I'm a lover
of what is: I love sickness and health, coming
and going, life and death. I see life and death
as equal. Reality is good. So death has to be
good, whatever it is, if it's anything at all.

The worst thing that can happen on your death bed are beliefs. Nothing worse than that has ever happened, ever.

The fear of death is the last smokescreen for the fear of love. We think that we're afraid of the death of our body, though what we're really afraid of is the death of our identity. But through inquiry, as we understand that death is just a concept and that our identity is a concept too, we come to realize who we are. This is the end of fear.

Loss is just a concept. I was in the delivery room when my grandson Race was born. I loved him at first sight. Then I realized that he wasn't breathing. The doctor had a troubled look on his face and immediately started to do something with the baby. The nurses realized that the procedures weren't working, and you could see the panic begin to take over the room. Nothing they did was working—the baby wouldn't breathe. At a certain moment, Roxann looked into my eyes, and I smiled. She later told me, "You know that smile you often have on your face? When I saw you look at me like that, a wave of peace came over me. And even though the baby wasn't breathing, it was okay with me."

Soon afterward, breath entered my grandson, and I heard him cry. I love that my grandson didn't have to breathe for me to love him. Whose business was his breathing? Not mine. I wasn't going to miss one moment of him, whether he was breathing or not. I knew that even without a single breath, he had lived a full life. I love reality, not the way a fantasy would dictate, but just the way it is, right now.

The great thing about death is that you do it on your own. Finally you get to do something completely on your own!

There's no decision in death. People who know that there's no hope are free. The decision's out of their hands. It has always been that way, but some people have to die bodily to find out. No wonder they smile on their deathbeds. Dying is everything they were looking for in life. Their delusion of being in charge is over. When there's no choice, there's no fear. And in that, there is peace. They realize that they're home and that they've never left.

Parents and relatives of children who have died are especially attached to their stories, for reasons that we all understand. Leaving our sadness behind, or even inquiring into it, may seem like a betrayal of our child. Many of us aren't ready to see things another way yet, and that's as it should be. It takes a great deal of courage to see through the story of a death.

Who thinks that death is sad? Who thinks that a child shouldn't die? Who thinks that they know what death is? Who tries to teach God, in story after story, thought after thought? Is it you? I say, let's investigate, if you're up for it, and see if it's possible to end the war with reality.

I have sat with many people on their deathbeds, and after we do The Work, they always tell me that they're fine. I remember one very frightened woman who was dying of cancer. She had requested that I sit with her, so I came. I sat down beside her and said, "I don't see a problem." She said, "No? Well, I'll show you a problem!" and she pulled off the sheet. One of her legs was so swollen that it was at least twice the size of the normal leg. I looked and I looked, and I still couldn't find a problem. She said, "You must be blind! Look at this leg. Now look at the other one." And I said, "Oh, now I see the problem. You're suffering from the belief that that leg should look like this one. Who would you be without that thought?" And she got it. She began to laugh, and the fear just poured out through her laughter. She said that this was the happiest she had ever been in her entire life.

If we see the death of a child and feel turmoil inside, it's the story we are telling that causes us pain. This is obvious. If a child dies and no one tells us, we don't feel a thing. A mother is crying somewhere at the loss of her child, and not knowing it, we sit here having a wonderful time. How heartless of us!

I once went to visit a woman who was dying in a hospice. When I walked in, she was napping, so I just sat by her bed until she opened her eyes. I took her hand, and we talked for a few minutes, and she said, "I'm so frightened. I don't know how to die." And I said, "Sweetheart, is that true?" She said, "Yes. I just don't know what to do." I said, "When I walked in, you were taking a nap. Do you know how to take a nap?" She said, "Of course." And I said, "You close your eyes every night, and you go to sleep. People look forward to sleeping. That's all death is. That's as bad as it gets, except for your belief system that says there's something else." She told me she believed in the after-death thing and said, "I won't know what to do when I get there." I said, "Can you really know that there's something to do?" She said, "I guess not." I said, "There's nothing you have to know, and it's always all right. Everything you need is already there for you; you don't have to give it a thought. All you have to do is take a nap when you need to, and when you wake up, you'll know what to do." I was describing life to her, of course, not death. Then we went into the second question of The Work, "Can you absolutely know that it's true that you don't know how to die?" She began to laugh and said that she preferred being with me to being with her story. What fun, having nowhere to go but where we really are now.

The questioned mind, because it's no longer seeking, is free to travel limitlessly. Thus it can never die. It understands that since it was never born, it has nothing to lose by allowing the unborn. It's infinite, because it has no desires for itself. It withholds nothing. It's unconditional, unceasing, fearless, tireless, without reservations. It has to give. That's its nature.

I have a friend who did inquiry sincerely for a number of years, and she really came to understand that the world was a reflection of her mind. She was married to a man who was the love of her life. And one day, while they were sitting on the couch together, he had a heart attack and died in her arms. After the first shock and the tears, she began looking for grief, and there was none. For weeks she kept looking for grief, because her friends told her that grief was a necessary part of the healing process. And all she felt was a completeness: that she was the same as her husband and he was the same as her, so that there was nothing she'd had while he was physically with her that she didn't have now. She told me that every time a sad thought about him appeared, she would immediately see the turnaround, which washed away the sadness and replaced it with what was truer.

"He was my best friend; I have no one to talk to now" became "I am my best friend; I have me to talk to now." "I'll miss his wisdom" became "I won't miss his wisdom"; there was no way she could miss it, because she *was* that wisdom. Everything she thought she'd had in him she could find in herself; there was no difference. And because he turned out to be her, he couldn't die. Without the story of life and death, she said, there was just love. He was always with her.

Until we know that death is as good as life, and that it always comes at just the right time, we're going to take on the role of God without the awareness of it, and it's always going to hurt. Whenever you mentally oppose what is, you're going to experience sadness and apparent separation. There's no sadness without a story. What is is. You *are* it.

Reality—the way that it is, exactly as it is, in every moment—is always kind. It's our *story* about reality that blurs our vision, obscures what's true, and leads us to believe that there is injustice in the world. I sometimes say that you move totally away from reality when you believe that there is a legitimate reason to suffer. When you believe that any suffering is legitimate, you become the champion of suffering, the perpetuator of it in yourself. It's insane to believe that suffering is caused by anything outside the mind. A clear mind doesn't suffer. That's not possible. Even if you're in great physical pain, even if your beloved child dies, even if you and your family are sent off to Auschwitz, you can't suffer unless you believe an untrue thought. I'm a lover of reality. I love what is, whatever it looks like. And however it comes to me, my arms are open.

It's our beliefs about death that scare us
to death.

Last year I was visiting Needles, the small
town in southern California where my
daughter lives. I was at the grocery store
with her when some old friends of the family
whom I hadn't seen for decades spotted me.
"Katie!" they called out, and they came up to
me, beaming. They hugged me, they asked
how I was, and then they asked, "And how
is your dear mother doing?" I said, "She's so
fine. She's dead." Suddenly the smiles were
gone. Silence. I saw that they were having
a problem, but I didn't know what it was.

Once Roxann and I were outside the store, she turned to me and said, "Mom, when you talk to people like that, they can't handle it." That hadn't occurred to me. I was just telling the truth.

Until you experience death as a gift, your work's not done. So if you're afraid of it, that shows you what to investigate next. There's nothing else to do; you're either believing these childish stories, or you're investigating them—there's no other choice. What's not okay about dying? You close your eyes every night, and you go to sleep. I don't see people worrying about sleep. People look forward to it; some people actually prefer that part. And that's as bad as it gets, except for your belief that says there's something else. Before a thought, there's no one, nothing—only peace that doesn't even recognize itself as peace. So when you go to sleep and you aren't dreaming, it's a sweet thing; you've left the confused dream we call life. And eventually, you can experience the same awareness, waking or asleep.

When you're clear about death, you can be totally present with someone who's dying, and no matter what kind of pain she appears to be

experiencing, it doesn't affect your happiness.
You just love her, you just hold her and care
for her, because it's your nature to do that. To
go to that person in fear is to teach fear: she
looks into your eyes and gets the message
that she is in deep trouble. But if you come in
peace, fearlessly, she looks into your eyes and
sees that whatever is happening is good.

Dying is just like living. It has its own way,
and you can't control it. People think, "I want
to be conscious when I die." That's hopeless.
Hopeless. Even wanting to be conscious ten
minutes from now is hopeless. You can only

be conscious now. Everything you want is here now.

I like to tell a story about a friend of mine who was on his death bed. He was very close to death, he thought, and trying to be completely conscious, and saving his energy, and waiting for a revelation. And finally his eyes widened, and he gasped, and he said, "Katie, we are larvae." Profound awareness on his deathbed. I said, "Sweetheart, is that true?" And the laughter simply poured out of him, and he got it, he said. The revelation was that there *was* no revelation. Things are fine just as they are. Only a concept can take that away from us. A few moments later he died, with a smile on his face.

A lover of what is looks forward to everything: life, death, disease, loss, earthquakes, bombs, anything the mind might be tempted to call "bad." Bring it all on, show me something that I haven't undone yet. Show me one thing outside myself that can make me suffer. Except for our unquestioned thoughts, every place is paradise.

My mother is dying of pancreatic cancer. I'm taking care of her, cooking and cleaning for her, sleeping beside her, living in her apartment twenty-three hours a day (my husband takes me out for one coffee break every morning). It has been a month now. It's as though her breath were the pulse of my life. I bathe her, I wash her in the most personal places, I medicate her, and I feel such a sense of gratitude. That's me over there, dying of cancer, spending my last few days sleeping and watching TV and talking, medicated with the most marvelous pain-killing drugs. I am amazed at the beauty and intricacies of her body, my body. And the last day of her life, as I sit by her bedside, a shift takes place in her breathing, and I know; it's only a matter of minutes now. And then another shift takes place, and I know. Our eyes lock, and a few moments later she's gone. I look more deeply into the eyes that the mind has vacated, the mindless eyes, the eyes of the no-mind, I wait for a change to take place. I wait for the eyes to show me death, and nothing changes. She's as present as she ever was. I love my story about her. How else could she ever have existed?

We could say that I've already died. What I know about it is that when there's no escape, when you know that no one is coming to save you, beliefs stop. You just don't bother. So if you are lying on your death bed and the doctor says it's all over for you and you believe him, all the confusion stops. There's no longer anything to lose. And in that sweet peace, there is only you. You are it, and that is presence.

Reality is the always-stable, never-disappointing base of experience. When I look at what really is, I can't find a me. As I have no identity, there's no one to die, therefore there's no one to resist death. Death is everything that has ever been dreamed, including the dream of myself, so at every moment I die of what has been and am continually born as awareness in the moment, and I die of that, and am born of it again. The thought of death excites me. It's done, I was absolute perfection, I could not have been lived a better life. And whatever I am is born in this moment as everything good that has ever lived.

Nothing was ever born but a dream. Nothing ever dies but a dream.